science

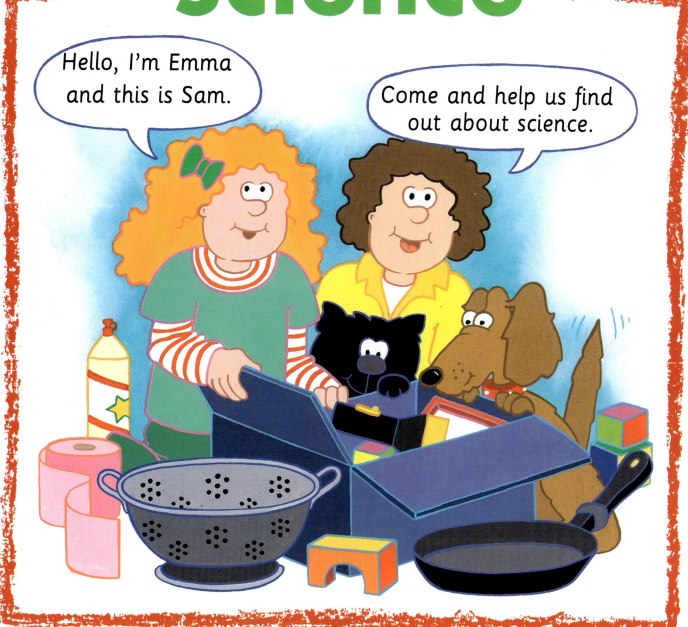

Linda Fisher

Illustrated by Karen Constantine

NOTES FOR PARENTS

Young children are natural scientists, as the endless 'how' and 'why' questions from them show. The activities in this book will encourage children to investigate their surroundings, to predict the possible results of their actions and to devise tests to check those results.

Try to answer any questions your child might have about the activities in this book as fully as possible. Don't be afraid to say if you don't know an answer. You and your child could find out together by doing an experiment or looking in a book. Encourage your child to think for him or herself by asking questions such as, 'What do you think would happen if…', 'Can you find out why it doesn't work?' or, 'Would it be better if you did it in a different way?'. Don't discourage your child's explanations of things, and accept them with a comment such as, 'Yes, it could be, couldn't it?' as they will seem logical to him or her. If your child is clearly wrong you could ask, 'Do you think there might be another reason?'.

Nurture your child's natural desire to learn; make finding out fun and your child will be eager to go to school and benefit from all that it has to offer.

Pages 4–5 Use your ears
Children rarely really listen. Encourage your child to use his or her ears and listen to the sounds in your surroundings. Talk about the different sizes and shapes of ears – animal and human!

Pages 6–7 Build a bridge
This game shows your child that materials have different strengths and weaknesses, which determine their suitability for use in a particular building situation.

Pages 8–9 Let's look at holes
Let your child decide for him or herself whether a hole is 'good' or 'bad'. The mousehole would probably be 'bad' to an adult, but from a child's point of view it could be 'good' because it is the mouse's home.

Pages 10–11 More holes
If your child enjoys doing this experiment, give him or her a sieve and some more ingredients, such as flour, for further investigation. Show your child how you use these utensils when cooking.

Pages 12–13 Be safe
The activity on this spread is a useful means of discussing safety with your child. Talk about your child's choices of what is dangerous and what is not. For example, wearing armbands in the swimming pool may be thought of as safe, but there should still be a grown-up nearby.

Pages 14–15 What a mess
Talk about pollution and get your child to help sort out newspapers and bottles for recycling.

Page 24 That's not right
In this activity your child will have to decide what is appropriate in a suitable situation.

Pages 16–17 Day and night
This is a simple activity to help your child think about time and the different things people do in the day and at night. Talk about your child's daily routine and the things that he or she does during the day which can't be done at night.

Pages 18–19 Torch light
This experiment demonstrates some of the properties of light. Your child could stand a small toy in front of the torch and make a shadow. If your child can't carry the light away on a sheet of paper, can he or she catch it in a box?

Pages 20–21 Bouncing lights
The activity on this spread is a continuation from the previous one. If you use the main room light or the sun rather than a torch do be careful that your child does not aim the reflections at anybody's eyes. Encourage your child to try to reflect the light off a non-shiny surface such as a 'towel'.

Pages 22–23 Reflections
What else can you and your child find to see yourselves in? Show your child how he or she can see you if you creep up behind him or her when he or she is looking in the mirror.

Use your ears

Look at the things in this picture.
Can you find the things that make a noise?
Draw a line from each noisy thing to Sam's ear.

Build a bridge

Sam and Emma are trying to build a bridge.
Can you help them?

Think of some of the bridges you have seen. Can you build a bridge of your own over the road on the next page?
Try to make your bridge strong enough for two of your toy cars to drive over.

Let's look at holes

Some holes are very useful but some are not.

Have a look at these holes.

If you think a hole is good, draw a 🙂 in the circle beside it.

If you think the hole is bad, draw a 🙁 instead.

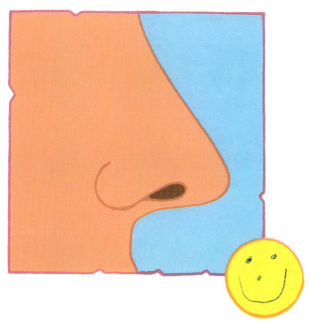

More holes

You need

- A colander
- A saucer of sultanas
- A saucer of sugar

Can you guess what will happen if you pour the sultanas into the colander?

Can you guess what will happen if you pour the sugar into the colander?

Now try it out.

Tick (✓) the pictures which show what happened.
Were you surprised?

Emma has got all the sultanas and sugar mixed up.
Can you think of a way to sort them out again?
Ask a grown-up to help you.

Be safe

Some things we can do by ourselves, but other things we need a grown-up to help us with.
Can you put a circle around all the dangerous things you must only do with a grown-up's help?

What a mess

Some very untidy people have been here.
Can you help the park keeper tidy up?

Look for the special place where all the rubbish should go.
Draw a line from each piece of rubbish to the special place for it.

Day and night

Here is a wide-awake day time picture.

Here is a sleepy night-time picture.

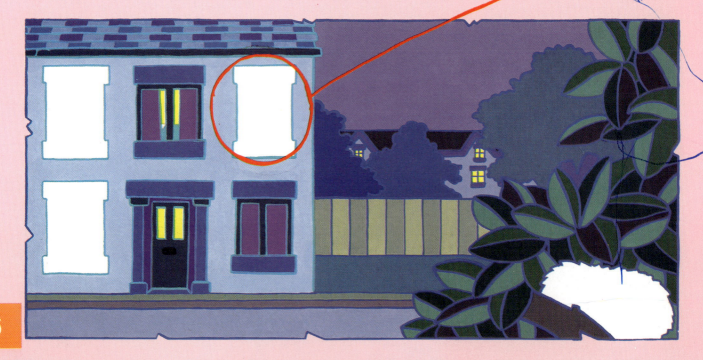

Can you sort out which of these things would happen in the day, and which would happen at night?

Draw a line from each small picture to the correct big picture.

I've done the first one.

Torch light

You need

A torch

A sheet of dark-coloured paper

Some coloured tissue or cellophane

1 Draw the curtains and turn off the lights so the room is quite dark.

2 Switch on the torch and put it on the table, so it makes a pool of light on the wall.

3 Now put a piece of coloured tissue or cellophane over the torch. What happens?

Try to catch the pool of light from the torch on the sheet of dark-coloured paper.

Can you move the paper and keep the light on it? Guess first, then try it.

Were you right?

Bouncing lights

You need

A torch

A shiny lid, such as a biscuit tin lid

This is a fun game to play.

Draw the curtains and turn off the lights so the room is quite dark.

Put the torch on the table and catch the light on the tin lid.

Now move the lid a little, and watch the light bounce off somewhere else.

Reflections

Have a look at yourself in the mirror.
Pull some funny faces and make yourself laugh.
Does the mirror-you laugh too?

Try touching your nose and ears.
Can you touch the nose and ears in the mirror?

Try making some different mirrors.
Ask a grown-up to help you.

1 Fill a dark-coloured shallow container, such as a non-stick frying pan, with water.

2 Wait until the water is quite still and then look in. Can you see yourself?

3 What happens if you touch your reflection?

4 Find a shiny spoon and look at yourself in both sides of it. What can you see?

Can you find any other things to use as a mirror?

That's not right

What a silly picture!
Put a cross (✗) on all the wrong things in the picture.

British Library Cataloguing in Publication Data
Fisher, Linda
 Science - (Headstart 3-5 Series)
 I. Title II. Series
 372.3

ISBN 0 340 57630 8
First published 1992
© 1992 Linda Fisher

All rights reserved. No part of this publication may be reproduced or transmitted in any form or by any means, electronic or mechanical, including photocopy, recording, or any information storage and retrieval system, without permission in writing from the publisher or under licence form the Copyright Licensing Agency Limited. Further details of such licences (for reprographic reproduction) may be obtained from the Copyright Licensing Agency Limited, of 90 Tottenham Court Road, London W1P 9HE.

Printed in Great Britain for the educational publishing division of Hodder & Stoughton Ltd, Mill Road, Dunton Green, Sevenoaks, Kent by Cambus Litho Ltd, East Kilbride.